For Robbie,
love you, yes I do
- Rachel x

A TEMPLAR BOOK

First published in the UK in 2012 by Templar Publishing,
an imprint of The Templar Company Limited,
The Granary, North Street, Dorking, Surrey, RH4 1DN, UK
www.templarco.co.uk

Copyright © 2012 by Rachel Bright

First edition

ISBN 978-1-84877-804-7

Printed in the U.K.

you make my heart go BOom

Tummy-jumbling little mini-WiSdOms On LOVE frOm

the bright side

verything

5

*Even the fluff in your Bellybutton

yes,
LOVe
(& Some Cool
AstroPhysicsy Stuff)

And you,
Wonderful you,
are

Out of this WORLD*

*In the Seriously-impressive-person
rather than Weird-green-alien way

Yes, you are

ONE
HOT
HUman

So to you, I dedicate this

LoVe Manifesto

I pledge to:

LOVe life itself

(the small things, the big things
& all the mediumy things).

To have Romantic
Cheeseboards for
dinner

& go all Spontaneous.

To listen to loVe Songs until I am actually crying

& polish my
Seduction routine
(til I can See my face in it).

I will Hold hands
& Snuggle Up.

I will
Go alfresco,
go à la carte,
go all impromptu,
go commando
& generally go for it with ALL my whole heart
(& other bodily bits)

&

Ooooooze Charm.

I will
Never settle for less than an
I'm-closing-my-eyes-&-punching-the-air
kind of love

&

I will
Be more together than
I could ever be on my own

& always try to look on
the bright side.

Yes, May LOVe FLiP you Over like a NiCely Browning pancake.*

*But may it not find you stuck on the Ceiling Or being half-eaten by the dog.

And remember…

Sometimes love can be a bit of…

a rollercoaster*

*One minute
you're screaming
your head off
& holding on for dear life.
the next you're thinking
"WoaHA!
That was fun."

A Love Song for You

Verse 1

(Emotional / Slightly starey-face)

OOOooooh You,
oOOOooh you,
You-oOOoo & Me-eeeee

CHORUS

(Grab air & get a bit shouty, quickly whip head
round to do starey face again)

You're like the Wind,
You're like the Skyyyyyyy,
You're like the moooOon,
I don't know whyyyyyyyy

verse 2

(stroke face & look wistful / voice goes a bit croaky)

And now my life is compleeeeete.
Are you feeling the Heeeaaaaat?
OoooooOh you-oooo
& Me-eeeeee...

Grand Finale

(Almost lost voice now / pelvic
thrust close eyes & punch air)

Make
Weeeeeeeeeeee*

*Not that kind of wee.

Yes, sometimes I just think

In fact, you might have to stop being so attractive... I can't get anything done.

*But you are usually doing something Weird, like riding a camel through the Frozen foods aisle shouting, "CHEESE IT!"

The Wonderful, weak-at-the-knees, oOOoooo

Birds Singing everywhere you go

Can't-eat-can't Sleep-can't-think-of-anything-else-lost-in-a-bubbleness

It feels permanently Sunny (even when it's not)

...it-sort-of-hurts-a-bit-in-my-heart, ♥

brilliant things about love being in the air:

Colours are the new black

Everyone's Smiling*

*even the usually grumpy people

The lyrics of love songs Suddenly making sense*

*except that Meatloaf One

Everything tastes Deeelicious... Everything Smells Wonderful*

*well almost everything

*& also
possibly cake.
Oh & definitely Slippers.
We all need slippers.
All you need is
love, cake & slippers.

...& a
kitten.
Just one tiny kitten
& then that's it.
I promise.

LOVe all things
(nOt juSt cute things like babieS & kittens)
& WHeN you
do love, LOVe
like They do in
PoWer Ballads.

(You know, like on a Cliff with the wind in your hair & your eyes shut, knowing you'll never know another love like this.)

THE END
(but also just the beginning)